A W·O·R·K·B·O·O·K O·F

Social Psychology

J.E. Alcock
GLENDON COLLEGE, YORK UNIVERSITY

D.W. Carment
McMASTER UNIVERSITY

S.W. Sadava
BROCK UNIVERSITY

Prentice-Hall Canada Inc., Scarborough, Ontario

Canadian Cataloguing in Publication Data

Alcock, James E.
  A workbook of social psychology

Supplement to: Alcock, James E. A textbook of
social psychology.
ISBN 0-13-912916-2

1. Social psychology. 2. Social psychology -
Problems, exercises, etc. I. Carment, D. W.,
1928-   . II. Sadava, S. W. III. Alcock, James E.
A textbook of social psychology. IV. Title.

HM251.A552 1988   302   C88-093974-5

Prentice-Hall, Inc., Englewood Cliffs, New Jersey
Prentice-Hall International, Inc., London
Prentice-Hall of Australia, Pty., Ltd., Sydney
Prentice-Hall of India Pvt., Ltd., New Delhi
Prentice-Hall of Japan, Inc., Tokyo
Prentice-Hall of Southeast Asia (Pte.) Ltd., Singapore
Editora Prentice-Hall do Brasil Ltda., Rio de Janeiro
Prentice-Hall Hispanoamericana, S.A., Mexico

ISBN 0-13-912916-2

Production Editor: Jessica Pegis
Coordinating Editor: Linda Gorman
Manufacturing Buyer: Matt Lumsdon

1 2 3 4 5   92 91 90 89 88

Printed and bound in Canada

Table of Contents

Introduction

The student who doesn't look at the text, or notes, until the night before an exam and yet achieves good marks is a rarity. For most students there is no shortcut to success in a course. Nor is there one proven method of study that works for everyone. However, there are a few principles which, if followed with reasonable diligence, will help to maximize the amount learned. We cannot go into great detail here but keep in mind that books on these topics are available in libraries and that counselling services offer advice and courses. Briefly, you should be concerned about the management of your time, the management of your workplace and the management of your learning strategies.

Time management involves setting schedules in which to fit all your activities both in the short-term (daily) and long-term (anticipating examinations and due dates for assignments). Also, time management requires the setting of priorities and being sensitive to those periods in the day when you operate most efficiently.

Obviously, studying has to occur in a physical location. The management of your workplace concerns how you deal with distractions (or potential distractions) and noise as well as the process of ensuring that you have regular access and that you have the appropriate equipment available.

This workbook is designed to be part of the third category, learning strategies. While there are a number of ways in which study can occur, one system which has proved effective for a lot of students is called the SQ3R method. SQ3R is mnemonic for Survey, Question, Read, Recall and Review, a sequential process that begins with a quick once-over of the chapter. This <u>Survey</u> allows you to note, in a general way, the headings and subheadings and the main points of the material. Next, turn each heading and subheading into a <u>Question</u>. This defines more precisely what it is you are to learn. Now <u>Read</u> the material in order to answer your questions. It is at this point that a hi-lighter can come in handy to underline the important pieces of information. Be selective, a book that is completely underlined is useless as a study tool. The next, and immediate, step is to <u>Recall</u> what you have read. Make notes so that you can check your recall with the text. Finally, what you have covered should be <u>Reviewed</u>. This doesn't mean re-reading the text. Go back over the notes you have made concentrating on the main points.

This workbook is designed to assist you in this process. For each chapter you will find a brief overview of main points that are covered. Then there is a list of <u>key terms</u> which you should learn. Record how many you correctly identify.

This is followed by 20 "fill-in-the-blank" questions that will test your recall as will the set of true-false items. Be sure in all cases that you keep track of your success rate. The answers are at the end of each chapter. The last section consists of short-answer questions which require a somewhat more elaborate response.

If you want to see how the principles discussed relate to "real life", we have supplied a list of relevant movies. Many of these are available in video cassette format and frequently appear on television. Watch your local listings.

Finally, we hope you find this book of help. Good luck and please write to us if you have questions, ideas, or criticisms.

Jim Alcock   **Toronto**
Bill Carment   **Hamilton**
Stan Sadava   **St. Catharines**

CHAPTER 2

Research and Research Methods

Overview

Social Psychology is a discipline which derives its knowledge from research based on the scientific method. This chapter briefly describes the nature of science and outlines how the scientific method differs from other ways of deriving conclusions about various phenomena. The role of theory in social psychology is discussed and the interplay between empirical research and theory is emphasized.

Social psychologists use a variety of means of obtaining data. Some of these are non-experimental which includes archival research, case studies, surveys, and field studies. Experimental methods are used in either the laboratory or the field. In this chapter we also discuss the difference between experimental and correlational approaches, we outline the importance of the statistics and we describe the process of statistical inference. Finally, we emphasize the importance of carrying out research in an ethical manner.

Define These Key Terms and Concepts

archival approach   p. 27

artifact (in an experiment)   p. 26

behaviourism   p. 20

control group post-test design   p. 40

correlation   p. 43-45

cross-cultural research   p. 37-38

debriefing   p. 47

Twenty Questions

1.   The scientific method depends on _____, _____,

          _____ and _____.

2.   The falsifiability of theory allows science to be _____

          _____.

3.   _____ is based on the premise that behaviour is governed

      by external reinforcement.

3

4. Lewin's field theory is an example of a _____ theory of social psychology.

5. In order to do scientific research on a phenomenon such as attitudes it is necessary to _____ that phenomenon.

6. If scores on a measure of attitudes toward political parties are influenced by the subjects' desire to create a good impression, that measure has a problem with _____ .

7. The _____ approach to research is non-reactive, can use data from a wide range of times and locations but does not allow for control over the quality of these data.

8. The survey method usually involves _____ measures.

9. The tendency of some subjects to agree or disagree with questionnaire items ("yea-sayers" and "nay-sayers") is one example of _____ .

10. The best way to ensure that subjects in various experimental conditions are undifferentiated before the experiment begins is by the _____ assignment of subjects to experimental groups.

11. Double-blind experimental designs are useful in avoiding both _____ and _____ effects.

12. When the behaviour of subjects in an experiment is influenced by what they believe to be the purpose of the study, the results of the study are affected by the _____ characteristics of the experiment.

13. If the situation in a laboratory experiment closely resembles one in the "real world", then that experiment can be described as having _____ realism and thus _____ validity.

14. The study by Doob and Gross (1968) of frustration and aggression in a traffic jam is a good example of research using the approach of a _____ _____.

15. The field experiment involves a trade-off of greater _____ for greater _____.

16. If we were to conduct a _____ in which we compared people's concerns about the weather in two cities, one of which had recently experienced a tornado, this would be a _____ design.

17. _____ procedures enable us to interpret research data.

18. The major advantage of a _____ is that we can study the effects of a major event that could not be produced in the laboratory.

19. When we compare sample means of scores from experimental and control groups, we want to ascertain whether any difference between them was likely to have been caused by the independent variable or occurred by _____.

20. _____, _____, and _____ are all ways of addressing concerns about the ethical problems of research.

True/False

1. Science deals with facts, not theory. ( )
2. Psychological constructs can only be inferred and not measured directly. ( )
3. The dependent variable is manipulated by the experimenter. ( )
4. Evidence from research proves whether a hypothesis is true or false. ( )
5. Experiment designs are best suited for the inference of cause and effect. ( )
6. A true experiment must have a least two groups of subjects. ( )
7. If an experiment is internally valid, it must be realistic and generalizable to the external world. ( )
8. In a quasi-experiment, the experimenter manipulates important variables. ( )
9. Statistical inference allows us to assess the real psychological significance of our results. ( )
10. A strong correlation means only that as scores on one variable increase, the scores on another variable also increase. ( )

Short Answer

1. What are the four basic characteristics of the scientific method?

2.   Outline the formal model of the scientific method.

3.   What are the attributes of a good measure, and how can we assess whether a measure is "good"?

4.   Outline the types of experimenter and subject effects which can produce artifacts in research.

5.   Contrast the experimental approach with the non-experimental approach to research.

6.   List the four non-experimental and three experimental research methods. Describe each. What are the advantages and disadvantages of each?

7.   What are the characteristics of a "true" experiment?

8.   What constitutes a "good" sample for research and how can it best be obtained?

ANSWERS

Twenty Questions

1. observation; hypothesis generation; hypothesis testing; replication
2. self-correcting
3. behaviourism
4. cognitive
5. operationalize
6. validity and/or social desirability
7. archival
8. self-report
9. response set
10. random
11. experimenter and subject
12. demand
13. mundane; high external
14. field experiment
15. external validity
16. quasi-experiment; control group post-test
17. statistical inference
18. quasi-experiment
19. chance
20. debriefing; informed consent; simulation

True/False

1. F
2. T
3. F
4. F
5. T
6. T
7. F
8. F
9. F
10. F

CHAPTER 3

Social Perception and Cognition

Overview

In the initial section of this chapter, we learn how a person forms an impression of someone else. There are several important biases which influence our impressions of others, such as that we tend to be more positive than negative in our impression of people. People combine information about various characteristics in order to arrive at an overall impression in accordance with a kind of mental averaging. While people form impressions of others, they also act to influence or "manage" the impression that others may form about them. We also look at how and when we can detect when someone is trying to deceive us.

The second section of the chapter turns to the processes of social cognition. We first discuss attributions, the inference of cause and effect, particularly in relation to how we arrive at a conclusion as to what causes someone to act in a certain manner. There are a number of theories to explain how we form causal attributions. Some pertain to how we decide whether a person's actions were caused by that person's own disposition or the situation in which the person was acting. Others deal with how we explain the cause of a success or failure, and how we decide whether a person is responsible for an outcome. Several important biases are discussed, including our tendency to ignore the role of the situation and to see people as the sole causes of their own actions, and a tendency to make attributions which protect our self-esteem. This leads to a discussion of the illusion of control, an exaggerated belief in the capacities of people to determine what happens to them. Finally, we examine the limits of attribution theories, those instances in which we are not concerned with understanding cause and effect. Research on thinking in terms of schemas serves to demonstrate how we make sense of our world rapidly and efficiently, if not always accurately or thoughtfully. This manner of rapid and almost automatic thinking influences processes of attention, memory and inference.

Define These Key Terms and Concepts

Twenty Questions

1. While people tend to be positive in their overall impressions
    of others, they tend to be influenced to a greater extent by
    _____ information.

2. The data from many studies on impression formation most
    strongly support a(n) _____ model of how we combine
    information.

3. In perceiving someone who is trying to hide their real feelings
    from us, we are better at detecting deception accurately than
    _____.

4. If a politician is friendly toward you at election time, you
    will tend to _____ the possibility that he or she really
    likes you.

5. In seminars, Sarah often argues with whatever you have just said. She also argues with others, while you have noticed that Rachel and Joanna generally agree with you. According to Kelley's covariation model, you are likely to attribute Sarah's behaviour to _____.

6. If someone behaves aggressively in a way that has personal consequences for you, you are likely to make a _____.

7. Weiner's model suggests that we judge achievement on the basis of a controllable, stable and _____ attribution.

8. We often are surprised by the results of studies which show the power of the situation upon people because of the

   _____.

9. We tend to make _____ attributions about our own actions, and _____ attributions about the actions of others.

10. In an experiment involving biases in attributions, some subjects simply reported attributions while others were hooked up to a "bogus pipeline" which would supposedly reveal their "true" feelings about those attributions. The results showed that, even when subjects believed that the machine would "give them away", they responded in a _____ manner.

11. Attributions of responsibility are influenced by the _____ of consequences.

12. People tend to blame victims for their fate because of a belief in a _____.

13. When an event is personally relevant, unexpected or important enough to impel a search for meaning, people are more likely to make _____.

14. In forming notions about categories of people or objects, we are often influenced by _____ of that category.

15. A prototype representing the attributes of members of a group is called a _____.

16. Studies of lay epistemology show that when there is time pressure or when there is a not any concern about the consequences of being wrong, our judgments tend to be subject to _____.

17. We have sets of interconnected beliefs, information and examples about social roles, events and people, including ourselves; these are called _____.

18. When we refer to a general schema about professors and specific schemata about professors of economics, Spanish literature, engineering and psychology, we are talking about an example of the _____ organization of schematic thinking.

19. We tend to be less able to recognize individuals from a race other than our own because of the effects of a(n) _____.

20. In an experiment, subjects who were asked to "imagine what it would be like" if a certain candidate won an election were more likely to predict that the candidate would win, reflecting the _____ heuristic.

True/False

1. We tend to be attracted to someone who is "hard-to-get". ( )
2. We are good in detecting what a person's "true" feelings are, even when they are trying to deceive us. ( )
3. In general, people who are depressed make stable external attributions. ( )
4. Regardless of what happens, we are predisposed to hold people responsible for their own actions and consequences. ( )
5. We tend to look for attributions when something that is unexpected happens. ( )
6. Because of schemas, we may see the past through rose-coloured glasses. ( )
7. Studies show that when we evaluate a group, we are strongly influenced by information about how typical a given example of that group may be. ( )
8. In forming impressions of people we tend to accentuate the positive and ignore negative information. ( )
9. The "Machiavellian" person is one who tends to make correspondent inferences about people. ( )
10. We tend to believe that we can control our environment and that people get what they deserve in life. ( )

Short Answer Questions

1. Describe an experiment (including method, important results) for each of the following: central traits, attribution about achievement, influence of schemata on memory, actions without conscious thought.

2. Outline the biases in attributions.

3. What are the five cues which influence us to make a correspondent inference?

4. Outline the Kelley covariation model.

5. What is the actor/observer bias and why does it occur?

6. Why do we have schemata?

7. Outline four types of schemata.

8. Describe the heuristic biases that influence our thinking.

9. How is our thinking influenced by priming and availability?

10. What are the limits of attribution theories in describing our way of thinking? When do we look for causes?

Social Psychological Cine

Being There (Hal Ashby, 1979)
Citizen Kane (Orson Welles, 1941)
Rashom'on (Akira Kurosawa, 1951)
Rear Window (Alfred Hitchcock, 1954)
Victor/Victoria (Blake Edwards, 1982)

ANSWERS

Twenty Questions

1. negative
2. weighted averaging model
3. leakage
4. discount
5. Sarah
6. correspondent inference
7. internal
8. fundamental attribution error
9. situational; dispositional
10. self-serving
11. severity
12. just world
13. attributions
14. prototypes
15. stereotype
16. freezing
17. schemata
18. hierarchical
19. illusory correlation
20. availability

True/False

1. T
2. F
3. T
4. F
5. T
6. T
7. F
8. F
9. F
10. T

CHAPTER 4

Attitudes and Values

Overview

In this chapter, we focus on social attitudes and on more broadly-based underlying values. Attitudes are described as an integrated set of feelings, beliefs and tendencies to behave in certain ways toward some person, object or issue, and can be measured through direct self-reported responses to questions or through various indirect techniques. Values refer to our global ideas of what is desirable or important in life, both in terms of certain end-states (freedom, comfort, independence) and in terms of how to attain valued goals, (being ambitious, imaginative, obedient). When people are impelled to examine their beliefs in relation to values, their attitudes (for example, the "pro-life" and "pro-choice" polarities in the abortion debate). The attitudes that people hold may reflect their values, but may also reflect unconscious conflicts, adaptation to social pressures or simply a need to understand their world.

We then turn to the important problem of how attitudes are related to behaviour. Evidence is reviewed to show that people often do not behave in a way consistent with their attitudes. This is particularly true when other attitudes may also be relevant to the behaviour in question, when other needs of the person are involved or when situational factors strongly influence the behaviour. A theory is presented which predicts that when a favourable attitude toward a certain action is accompanied by the perception that others are in agreement, that attitude will lead to behaviour.

Define These Key Terms and Concepts

attitude	p. 96
bogus pipeline	p. 98
conditioned semantic generalization	p. 98

Twenty Questions

1. Since an attitude can only be inferred and never directly
    observed, attitude is a _____ .

2. Attitudes vary in their _____, the degree to which the issue or object is important to the individual.

3. The tripartite model of attitudes consists of three components, which are _____, _____, and _____.

4. The tripartite model of attitudes implies that our thoughts, feelings and actions are _____ in some way.

5. _____ values are preferences for certain end-states in life, while _____ values represent preferred modes of conduct.

6. People of various political ideologies differ in how they rank the values of _____ and _____.

7. When the relative values placed on freedom and equality were discussed with subjects in the Rokeach study of value _____, they later were more likely to join a civil rights organization.

8. When people are faced with an issue that involves competing values, they are more likely to engage in _____, (considering all sides of the issue).

9. In a study comparing values of subjects in many different nations (Hofstede, 1985), one important dimension was _____, the extent that people believe they can control and be controlled by others.

10. An attitude serving an instrumental function enables us to gain
_____ from others.

11. An attitude may serve a knowledge function, acting as a
_____ to determine reactions without involving thought.

12. A study by Kristiansen and Zanna (1986) shows that attitudes
are related to the expression of values when the attitude is
linked to the _____ of a valued goal.

13. One reason why advocates of opposing sides of a contentious
issue cannot communicate effectively is because they are
appealing to different _____.

14. The LaPiere (1934) study of hotels and restaurants which either
were or were not willing to provide service to a Chinese couple
was an unsuccessful attempt to study the relationship of
_____.

15. A person's behaviour may not be consistent with a particular
attitude because the behaviour is relevant to other
_____.

16. The most prominent theory relating attitudes to behaviour is
the theory of _____.

17. The Fishbein and Ajzen theory of reasoned action states that
the best predictor of an action is _____.

18. In the theory of reasoned action, the attitude toward a(n)

    _____ is determined by a belief that the action will

    lead to a given consequence.

19. The most widely used method of attitude measurement is

    _____, in which subjects respond to statements along a

    scale of 5 or 7 points.

20. Indirect measures do not involve direct _____ of the

    person's attitudes.

True/False

1. Surprisingly, most people tend not to rate health as an important value. ( )
2. People with conservative beliefs value freedom more highly than equality, while leftists value equality more than freedom. ( )
3. Integrative complexity tends to be higher among people with conservative political ideologies. ( )
4. Canadians tend to value self-control, obedience and being ambitious more highly than people in the United States. ( )
5. Contemporary studies show that French Canadians place less value on achievement and independence than English-speaking Canadians. ( )
6. Since value is a higher-order concept, values can predict attitudes but attitudes cannot predict values. ( )
7. Research shows consistently that attitudes accurately predict behaviour. ( )
8. In general, indirect measures of attitudes are much more effective than self-reports. ( )
9. As a person has more experience and greater involvement with an activity, attitudes become more complex. ( )
10. The research on the theory of reasoned actions shows clearly that attitudes predict intentions but not behaviour. ( )

Short Answer Questions

1. What are the differences between attitudes and values?

2. How are values related to political ideologies?

3. Outline the four functions of attitudes.

4. Describe four value dimensions along which differences between nations have been studied.

5. Compare citizens of Canada and the U.S.A. in terms of values.

6. Outline the personal and situational factors which determine the relationship between attitudes and behaviour.

7. Outline and criticize the theory of reasoned action.

8. What is the difference between direct and indirect attitude measurement? Describe three examples of each.

Social Psychology Cine

Breaking Away (Peter Yates, 1979)
Decline of the American Empire (Denys Arcand, 1986)
Inherit the Wind (Stanley Kramer, 1960)
Love and Death (Woody Allen, 1974)
Midnight Cowboy (John Schlesinger, 1969)
Nobody Waved Goodbye (Don Owen, 1964)
Room at the Top (Jack Clayton, 1959)
Rules of the Game (Jean Renoir, 1939)
The Boys in the Band (William Friedkin, 1970)
The Gods Must be Crazy (Jamie Uys, 1985)
The Informer (John Ford, 1935)
The Revolutionary (Paul Williams, 1970)

ANSWERS

Twenty Questions

1. hypothetical construct
2. centrality
3. cognitive; affective; behavioural
4. integrated
5. terminal; instrumental
6. freedom; equality
7. confrontation
8. trade-off reasoning
9. power distance
10. acceptance or approval
11. schema
12. attainment
13. values
14. attitudes and behaviour
15. attitudes
16. reasoned action
17. an intention
18. action
19. Likert summated ratings
20. self-reports

True/False

1. F
2. T
3. F
4. F
5. F
6. F
7. F
8. F
9. T
10. F

CHAPTER 5

Attitude Change

Overview

In this chapter, the focus on attitudes is shifted to the processes by which people change their attitudes. Attitude change as an internal process is discussed within the framework of cognitive dissonance theory, based on the premise that changes in attitudes are impelled by the perception that we are being inconsistent in our attitudes or actions. Dissonance is aroused in certain situations, such as after we must make a difficult choice, when we are exposed to contrary information, or when we act in a certain way despite having attitudes to the contrary. Dissonance has been shown to be a genuine state of arousal, which occurs when one has acted in counter-attitudinal ways with free choice and without external justification, and where a sense of discomfort is attributed to this state of dissonance. That is, if we feel that we were forced to do something contrary to our beliefs, or if we feel that we acted in this way to gain some valued external reward, we will not experience cognitive dissonance.

Attitudes often change in response to external influences. To some extent, attitudes may be subject to processes of classical conditioning. More often, people are persuaded to change their attitudes as a result of a number of interacting factors: the credibility and attractiveness of the person who tries to persuade us, the nature of the message itself (primacy or recency, whether it arouses fear), the nature of the target or audience for the message and whether the message is conveyed verbally, visually or in written form. People can best resist attempts to persuade them when they are forewarned of the attempt to persuade or when previously exposed to arguments against their position ("inoculation"). In general, persuasion can occur by two principle routes: the central route in which the person is stimulated to think about the issues, and the peripheral route in which the attractiveness or distracting nature of the message or source lead to more superficial changes. The former is both uncommon and more enduring.

Define These Key Terms and Concepts

Twenty Questions

1. The _____ principle underlies much of the theory and
    research on the cognitive processes involved in attitude
    change.

2. According to the theory of cognitive dissonance, two cognitions may have a(n) _____, _____, or _____ relationship with each other.

3. The ratio of dissonant to consonant cognitions and the importance of each cognition determine the

   _____.

4. Bolstering, rationalizing and changing behaviour are ways of

   _____.

5. In the study of post-decision dissonance, it was found that we may experience a short-term _____ in which we undervalue the choice made and overvalue the rejected alternative.

6. The arousal of post-decision dissonance is strongly influenced by whether the person had a(n) _____.

7. The study by Festinger, Riecken and Schachter (1956) of members of a "doomsday cult", who were awaiting a spaceship, illustrates the role of _____ in cognitive dissonance.

8. When people engage in attitude-discrepant behaviour, the extent to which they experience cognitive dissonance will depend primarily on _____ for their action.

9. In the "forbidden toy" experiment, children who were told that the experimenter would merely be "annoyed" with them came to be _____ attracted to that toy than those threatened with the anger of the experimenter and with losing access to all of the toys.

10. The Cooper, Zanna and Taves (1978) experiment showed that attitude-discrepant behaviour led to greater attitude change when subjects were administered an amphetamine, but less when given a tranquilizer. This experiment supports the notion that cognitive dissonance is a state of _____.

11. The self-perception model of attitude change states that the effects of attitude-discrepant behaviour on subsequent attitudes depends on our _____ about our own behaviour.

12. If children acquire an attitude toward some group because mention of that group is always accompanied by expressions of negative feelings by their parents, this would illustrate the role of _____.

13. If a source of a communication is perceived as expert or trustworthy, that source will be _____.

14. Low to intermediate fear arousal tends to be _____ related to attitude change, and high fear arousal to be _____ related to attitude change.

15. The effects of forewarning on resistance to persuasion rest on the perception of the source's _____ to persuade and on knowing about the content of the message.

16. The _____ effect suggests that children should be exposed to a full range of opinions on all kinds of issues if they are to be resistant to persuasion.

17. According to Kelman, compliance does not lead to attitude change unless the person _____ with the communicator or _____ the message.

18. In general research shows that women are not more easily _____ than men.

19. Relatively enduring and "real" attitude change is more likely when accompanied by _____ about the issue.

20. Most television commercials are directed to the _____ route of persuasion.

True/False

1. Cognitive dissonance often occurs before we make a difficult decision. ( )
2. When people are given large bribes to say something that they don't believe, they are likely to change their attitudes. ( )
3. When cognitive dissonance occurs, it is a state of emotional arousal. ( )
4. Evidence suggests that dissonance effects are strongest when linked to the person's self-concept. ( )
5. If series of arguments immediately follow one after the other, then the argument presented last in the sequence will have the most impact. ( )

6. A difficult or complicated message will have a greater impact when presented in written form, while an easy-to-understand message will be more persuasive on television. ( )
7. If you want children to develop strong beliefs about right and wrong, then you should restrict the range of ideas to which they are exposed. ( )
8. People are more able to resist attempts to persuade them if they are first made aware that the attempt will be made. ( )
9. Research shows clearly that through socialization, women are more easily persuaded than men. ( )
10. A novel or humorous communication from an attractive source is more likely to produce lasting attitude change than a communication which leads people to think about the issue. ( )

Short Answer Questions

1. Outline five ways to reduce cognitive dissonance.

2. Outline four different types of cognitive dissonance.

3. Under what conditions does attitude-discrepant behaviour lead to attitude change?

4. Outline the Cooper and Fazio integrated model of cognitive dissonance.

5. What four basic questions are posed in your text's analysis of persuasion? Give examples of each.

6. How and when does fear arousal lead to attitude change?

7. Describe an experiment which shows how persuasion may be resisted.

8. Outline Kelman's three-level model of how behavioural compliance may be related to attitude change.

9. Describe an experiment which shows how some combination of source, message, channel and audience characteristics act together to influence persuasion.

10. Outline the elaboration-likelihood model and indicate how it integrates much of what we know about attitude change.

Social Psychological Cine

Angels with Dirty Faces (Michael Curtiz, 1938)
Inherit the Wind (Stanley Kramer, 1960)
Prelude to War (Frank Capra, 1942)
The Best of Enemies (Guy Hamilton, 1962)
The Seventh Seal (Ingmar Bergman, 1957)
Triumph of the Will (Leni Riefenstahl, 1936)

ANSWERS

Twenty Questions

1. consistency
2. consonant; dissonant; irrelevant
3. magnitude of dissonance
4. reducing dissonance
5. regret phase
6. free choice
7. social support
8. external justification
9. less
10. arousal
11. attributions
12. classical conditioning
13. credible
14. positively; negatively
15. intent
16. inoculation
17. identifies; internalizes
18. influenced
19. thinking
20. peripheral

True/False

1. F
2. F
3. T
4. T
5. F
6. T
7. F
8. T
9. F
10. F

CHAPTER 6

Social Influence and Conformity

Overview

Individuals influence one another in a variety of ways. The most basic form of social influence is due to the mere presence of others. This is called social facilitation and, depending on whether learning or performance is involved, can either improve or impair behaviour. Why this occurs has been the subject of considerable research that has implicated arousal, evaluation apprehension and distraction - conflict as important factors. Another effect of the presence of others is called social loafing. This is when individuals, working together, put less effort into a task than they each would if alone.

This chapter also points out that people often change their behaviour and beliefs and attitudes so as to be similar to others. Thi is conformity and it serves a number of purposes. It is rewarding, it assists in testing reality and it can be used as a social tactic. While it is difficult to resist pressures to conform those who do are often able to influence the majority.

Direct methods of modifying behavior result in compliance. Among the methods deliberately used to obtain compliance are the foot-in-the-door, the door-in-the-face and the low ball techniques. Improving-the-deal, thats-not-all, as well as instigating guilt are other compliance tactics. Obedience occurs when a person responds to a direct request from someone with authority.

The chapter also includes a discussion of some of the dangers of excessive conformity such as group-think and the stifling of innovative thought and action.

Define These Key Terms and Concepts

Twenty Questions

1. Early research in social psychology by Triplett dealt with how
    performance is influenced by the presence of others without

    _____ .

2. The phenomenon described above is called _____ .

Behaviour is facilitated by the presence of others when the behaviour is

_____.

. Social facilitation may deal with _____ effects, when others are

observing the person, or _____ effects, when others are

performing the same task independently and simultaneously.

. Zajonc explains the differing effects of the presence of others on

performance in terms of _____.

. Cottrell explains the effects of the presence of others in terms of

_____ rather than as a biological drive.

. Social loafing is defined as a decrease in _____ in the

presence of other coactors.

. In Sherif's work on individual judgments of the autokinetic effect, he

proposed that individuals arrive at a common _____ about the

behaviour.

. In an experiment (Moscovici et al., 1974), two confederates in groups of

six subjects identified shades of blue as green; this

_____ influenced responses by subjects.

. Groups tend to be more accepting of non-conformity from high-status

group members because of their _____ credits.

. In cases where there is ambiguity or no demonstrably correct answer,

people tend to engage in social _____.

12. If people are more likely to put up a lawn poster after first signing petition for the same cause, compliance has been elicited through the _____ technique.

13. The door-in-the-face technique is effective because of _____ and _____.

14. _____ involves requests to act, and _____ involves dema to act.

15. Social modelling is a process of _____ social influence.

16. When we observe a model reacting positively to the positive consequen of behaviour, and we experience something of that reaction, then we experience _____ reinforcement.

17. The results of telethons for various charities are examples of the _____ effects of modelling.

18. Janis' analysis of group think states that certain groups are very concerned with protecting group _____ and avoiding _____ influences.

19. Strickland's research show that _____ tends to make us less trusting of those whom we subject to it.

20. The two-step flow of communication involves the diffusion of innovati from _____ to others.

True/False

1. When we must study new material in our social psychology course, the presence of others will help us to learn it. ( )

2.	Social facilitation does not occur unless people believe that others are watching and evaluating them. ( )
3.	In the Asch experiments, conformity was elicited if a majority of confederates first gave the wrong response. ( )
4.	Pressure to conform increases as the size of the group increases independently. ( )
5.	Minority influence is more likely than majority influence to produce real attitude change, rather than just conformity. ( )
6.	Compliance, even for the demands of an uninvolved third-party, becomes more likely when guilt has been aroused. ( )
7.	In Milgram's experiment on obedience to authority, almost one in three subjects obeyed fully. ( )
8.	In group think conditions, all potential solutions are considered and outside opinions are invited. ( )
9.	Group brainstorming is not demonstrably superior to individual brainstorming for arriving at creative ideas and solutions. ( )
10.	Many of the worst acts of aggression have more in common with social influence than with instigators of aggression. ( )

Short Answer Questions

1.	Research on social facilitation shows that the effects on performance may be positive or negative. How does Zajonc explain this apparent contradiction and what is Cottrell's alternative explanation?

2.	Describe an experiment on reactions to conformity and deviation in a discussion group, and explain the results.

3.	Outline five reasons for conformity.

4. Describe five situations which influence compliance.

5. Describe the Milgram study on obedience, the processes involved and th major findings.

6. Describe the influence of reference groups.

7. Outline Bandura's theory of modelling.

8. What are the "symptoms" and the consequences of group think?

9. How can innovation be promoted and diffused?

10. What do experiments show regarding gender differences in conformity an why?

Social Psychological Cine

A High Wind in Jamaica (Alexander MacKendrick, 1965)
All the King's Men (Robert Rossen, 1949)
Breaker Morant (Bruce Beresford, 1979)
Conduct Unbecoming (Michael Anderson, 1975)
Diner (Barry Levinson, 1982)
I'm All Right, Jack (John and Ray Boulting, 1960)
Judgement at Nuremberg (Stanley Kramer, 1961)
Man in the Grey Flannel Suit (Nunnally Johnson, 1956)
Merry Christmas, Mr. Lawrence (Nagisa Oshima, 1982)
One Flew Over the Cuckoo's Nest (Milos Forman, 1975)
Room at the Top (Jack Clayton, 1959)
The Blackboard Jungle (Richard Brooks, 1955)
The Caine Mutiny (Edward Dmytryk, 1954)
The World According to Garp (George Roy Hill, 1982)
Tunes of Glory (Ronald Neame, 1960)

ANSWERS

Twenty Questions

1. interaction
2. social facilitation
3. simple or well-learned
4. audience; coaction
5. arousal
6. evaluation apprehension
7. individual effort
8. norm
9. adamant minority
10. idiosyncrasy
11. comparison
12. foot-in-the-door
13. reciprocal concession; self-presentation
14. compliance; obedience
15. unintentional
16. vicarious
17. response facilitation
18. solidarity; outside
19. surveillance
20. opinion-leaders

True/False

1. F
2. F
3. F
4. F
5. T
6. T
7. F
8. F
9. T
10. T

CHAPTER 7

Prejudice, Discrimination, and Sexism

Overview

Prejudice and discrimination are problems most societies experience. In this chapter prejudice is considered in terms of three basic components: cognitive (stereotypes), affective (emotions), and behavioural (discrimination). The discussion of stereotypes focuses on their persistence and pervasiveness and how they are measured, which leads to the question of the accuracy of stereotypes. While most stereotypes are overgeneralizations and are inaccurate, situational pressures sometimes makes stereotypes "come true".

The behavioural element of prejudice, discrimination, can to some extent be legally controlled but subtle forms of discrimination continue to exist. Reverse discrimination occurs when people behave so as to imply that they are considerably more tolerant than they really are. Generally, reverse discrimination is restricted to relatively trivial actions and may not lead to long-lasting tolerance.

Prejudice is acquired through learning with the parents playing an early crucial role. In some cases this early experience may lead some people to exhibit characteristics of the authoritarian personality. These individuals, who are prejudiced and ethnocentric, can exhibit considerable hostility towards "out-groups". Teachers and experience in the classroom also can, either directly or indirectly, contribute to the acquisition of prejudice as can the media and those with whom the child associates in peer groups. Clearly the reduction of prejudice is important. Tolerance can be increased by interethnic contact as long as certain conditions, such as equality of status, favourable circumstances, and interdependent goals, are met. Unfortunately, the positive effects of intergroup contact are often restricted to the group members and are not generalized to the larger community. It is also the case that, because of intergroup anxiety, getting people to interact with the members of other groups may be difficult.

One of the most reliable ways of decreasing prejudice is through education. Research is consistent in demonstrating that those with higher levels of education are more tolerant.

Those who are the victims of prejudice may react in a number of ways which can range from self-hate and withdrawal to collective action. Among those who experience prejudice, the largest group is women. Women are often stereotyped as inferior to men and many occupations are sex-typed, with women assigned to jobs with lower status and lower pay.

Define These Key Terms and Concepts

Twenty Questions

1. Prejudice is a(n) _____ with cognitive, affective and behavioural components.

2. The cognitive component of prejudice consists of _____.

3. The evidence on stereotypes is that they are relatively stable _____ over time but vary according to circumstances.

4. Dutton's experiment, in which certain minorities were permitted to violate formal dress requirements in restaurants, demonstrates the phenomenon of _____.

5. While stereotypes often are not accurate, they may have a degree of validity because of the _____.

6. Stereotypes are commonly measured by an _____ checklist.

. Research on beliefs about U.S. Blacks, which found that the diagnostic ratio for undesirable characteristics is more extreme than the criterion ratio, casts doubt on the _____ hypothesis.

. Stereotypes are often maintained through a cognitive bias in processing information, called the _____.

. The behavioural component of prejudice is called _____.

. When discrimination is supported by laws or other regulations or practices in society, it is _____.

.. The _____ hypothesis states that positive feelings toward other groups are related to feelings of security in one's own cultural identity.

2. The _____ effect is consistent with Hebb's view that there is an innate fear of the unfamiliar.

3. Prejudice is acquired through processes of _____ and _____ conditioning and _____.

4. The _____ personality tends to be prejudiced.

5. When members of a minority group are blamed for social or economic ills of society, that group has been made a _____.

6. Intergroup contact leads to reduced prejudice when members of each group are of _____ status or the _____ group is of higher status.

17. Studies of intercultural visits show that those who emerge with favourable attitudes are those who were _____ before the visit and who reported more frequent _____ with the other group.

18. Intergroup anxiety often is based on expectations of negative _____ or _____ consequences for the self.

19. Allport describes _____ and _____ reactions by the victims of prejudices.

20. Many of the stereotypes about males and females pertain to _____ of the two sexes.

True/False

1. Prejudice refers to racial or religious differences. ( )
2. Reverse discrimination tends to occur only in relatively unimportant situations. ( )
3. Most studies show that stereotypes carry some degree of truth: "where there's smoke, there's fire." ( )
4. The evidence strongly indicates that prejudice is based on an inherent fear and distrust of those who are different. ( )
5. Research on certain characteristics of personality suggests that not everyone is equally prone to prejudice. ( )
6. Research on the effects of presenting a comical, bigoted character on (All in the Family) shows that such programs may actually strengthen prejudice in those already inclined in that way. ( )
7. Intergroup contact usually leads to less prejudice than if the groups are kept apart. ( )
8. Opportunities for intergroup contact do not always reduce prejudice because people will not take advantage of those opportunities. ( )
9. Cook's "railroad game" showed that intergroup contact reduced prejudice in a substantial minority of previously bigoted subjects. ( )
10. The experience of prejudice invariably results in adverse effects on the self-esteem of the victims. ( )

Short Answer Questions

1. What are stereotypes and how do they influence the way we relate to people?

2. How can we evaluate the pervasiveness, persistence and accuracy of stereotypes?

3. Evaluate the kernel of truth hypothesis about stereotypes, including work on the "diagnostic ratio".

4. What is the multiculturalism hypothesis? Evaluate the relevant evidence.

5. What are the stages by which prejudice is socialized in the child?

6. What characteristics and processes of personality are related to prejudice?

7. What is the intergroup contact hypothesis and under what conditions i. it true?

8. Why does intergroup contact not always serve to disconform negative stereotypes, even when there is no truth to the stereotypes?

9. Outline Taylor and McKirnon's five-stage model of how members of grou, deal with prejudice.

10. What are the effects of gender role stereotypes, particularly in employment opportunities?

Social Psychological Cine

A Soldier's Story (Norman Jewison, 1985)
Birth of a Nation (D.W. Griffith, 1915)
Broken Arrow (Delmar Daves, 1950)
Fox and his Friends (Fraustrecht der Freiheit) (Rainer Fassbinder, 1975)
Gentleman's Agreement (Elia Kazan, 1947)
Guess Who's Coming to Dinner (Stanley Kramer, 1967)
In a Year of Thirteen Moons (Rainer Fassbinder, 1978)
Shoah (Claude Lanzmann, 1985)
Tea and Sympathy (Vincente Minnelli, 1956)
The Boys in the Band (William Friedkin, 1970)
The Elephant Man (David Lynch, 1980)
The Music Lovers (Ken Russell, 1970)

To Kill a Mockingbird (Robert Mulligan, 1962)
Tootsie (Sydney Pollack, 1982)
Voyage of the Damned (Stuart Rosenberg, 1976)

ANSWERS

Twenty Questions

1. attitude
2. stereotypes
3. change
4. reverse discrimination
5. self-fulfilling prophecy
6. adjective
7. kernel of truth
8. illusory correlation
9. discrimination
10. institutionalized
11. multiculturalism
12. mere exposure
13. classical; instrumental; modelling
14. authoritarian
15. scapegoat
16. equal; minority
17. favourable; contact
18. psychological; behavioural
19. intropunitive; extrapunitive
20. role-assignments

True/False

1. F
2. T
3. F
4. F
5. T
6. T
7. F
8. T
9. T
10. F

CHAPTER 8

Interpersonal Attraction and Interpersonal Relationships

Overview

In this chapter, we focus upon how and why we become attracted to others and on how close relationships develop over time. Human beings manifest a strong need to be with others (affiliation), rooted in their experiences of attachment in early childhood, and influenced by certain situations such as those which arouse fear. However, we are also selective about whom we want to be with; who we are attracted to depends on the relationship involved. We tend to be initially attracted to people who live or work in close physical proximity to ourselves and who are physically attractive. When we begin to interact, attraction is increased when we perceive that the person's attitudes, values and interests are similar to our own, and when the interaction has been rewarding to us in some way.

When a relationship can be described as being close or intimate, other factors come into play. Communicating about ourselves, contributes to the feeling of intimacy when it occurs reciprocally. A sense of equity or fairness contributes to the growth of intimacy and satisfaction in a relationship, although this sense of equity is no longer tied to an immediate quid pro quo exchange. Such relationships may be experienced as involving love, a blend of intense emotional involvement, commitment and intimacy. In social psychology, we study love as it is experienced and defined by those involved, perhaps even resulting from a misattribution of emotional arousal.

Relationship problems have also been studied. Marital separation is an extremely stressful experience for most people, particularly for males. Jealousy may involve a desire for exclusivity in a relationship or a desire to compare oneself favourably with others, and invariably involves the perception of threat. Loneliness results from the perception of deficiencies in relationships rather than physical "aloneness", and from an internal and stable attribution for these deficiencies. Shyness is sometimes related to loneliness, and can be treated behaviourally.

Define These Key Terms and Concepts

Twenty Questions

1. _____ begins in early infancy, when the infant can distinguish familiar faces.

2. Situations which arouse fear tend to increase affiliative behaviour, because of our need to _____ our reaction with that of others.

3. The graduate students' apartment study demonstrates the effect of _____ on attraction.

4. When we see a very attractive and admirable person commit a blunder our liking for that person tends to _____.

5. The effect of _____ on attraction can be explained in terms of opportunities for interaction, expectations for continued encounters and mere exposure.

6. Newcomb's longitudinal study of students in a university rooming house demonstrates the importance of _____ on initial attraction.

7. Byrne's law states that attraction increases with the _____ of similar attitudes.

8. One explanation of the similarity-attraction relationship is that, when we like someone, we expect that they will be _____.

9. Byrne and Clore's reinforcement-affect model states that we like people whom we _____ with reward, even if they were not the source of the reward.

10. Aronson has shown that we like someone who becomes more attracted to us over time than someone who constantly likes us; this is called the _____ effect.

11. Self-disclosure is an important indicator of _____ in a relationship.

12. Altman and Taylor's model of social penetration describes self-disclosure in terms of _____ and _____.

13. Altman and Taylor state that relationships involve a changing balance between concerns for _____ and

_____ .

14. Foa's model of social exchange postulates six interpersonal resources which are described in terms of

_____ and _____ .

15. In intimate relationships, social exchanges become more _____ and less concerned with _____ reciprocation.

16. _____ is the principle that opposites attract.

17. Research shows that passionate love in the early stages of a relationship tends to evolve into _____ love.

18. In research on jealousy, it is important to distinguish between the desire for _____ in a relationship and the desire to feel superior to someone else.

19. Loneliness involves the perception that one's relationships are _____ in some way, regardless of the presence or absence of other people.

20. Dispositionally lonely people tend to attribute their loneliness to _____ and _____ causes.

True/False

1. Research shows that misery loves company which is equally miserable. ( )
2. According to research data, people generally act on the principle that "you can't judge a book by its cover" with respect to attractiveness. ( )
3. The physical attractiveness effect is found primarily with regard to adult heterosexual attraction, and rarely among children. ( )
4. People tend to seek out others who have the most attractive characteristics, regardless of their own characteristics. ( )
5. We tend to be attracted to people who reward us. ( )
6. Apart from similarity, attractiveness, or other factors, interaction by itself can affect liking. ( )
7. When we anticipate having to interact with someone who is obnoxious, we tend to dislike that person more. ( )
8. Argyle and Dean show that, as self-disclosure increases or personal distance decreases, other reactions such as eye contact increase. ( )
9. Males tend to be more realistic or pragmatic in their attitudes toward romantic love. ( )
10. Males tend to suffer more adverse effects from divorce than females. ( )

Short Answer Questions

1. Name and briefly discuss two variables involved in each of Levinger and Snoek's stages of relatedness.

2. Apart from sexual attraction, how can the influence of physical attractiveness upon attraction be explained?

3. Outline three explanations for the relationship between similarity and attraction.

4. Describe Altman and Taylor's social penetration model, including the factor of privacy.

5. How is the equity principle applied to social exchange in committed relationships?

6. What is the sequential filter theory of relationship development?

7. Describe six (or more) characteristics of intimacy in relationships.

8. What is the triangular theory of love, and how do males and females differ in how they experience romantic love?

9. What is the relationship between passionate love and attributions?

10. Outline a model of jealousy.

Social Psychological Cine

Annie Hall (Woody Allen, 1977)
Brief Encounter (David Lean, 1946)
Butch Cassidy and the Sundance Kid (George Roy Hill, 1969)
Casablanca (Michael Curtiz, 1942)
Come Back Little Sheba (Daniel Mann, 1952)
Faithfully Yours (Preston Sturgis, 1948)
Hannah and Her Sisters (Woody Allen, 1986)
Kramer versus Kramer (Robert Benton, 1979)
Last Tango in Paris (Bernardo Bertolucci, 1973)
Marty (Paddy Chayefsky, 1955)
Montenegro (Dusan Makavejev, 1981)
Scenes from a Marriage (Ingmar Bergman, 1973)
Separate Tables (Delbert Mann, 1958)
The Goodbye Girl (Herbert Ross, 1977)
The Servant (Joseph Losey, 1963)
Woman in a Dressing Gown (J. Lee Thompson, 1957)

ANSWERS

Twenty Questions

1. attachment
2. compare
3. propinquity
4. increase
5. propinquity
6. similarity
7. proportion
8. similar to ourselves
9. associate
10. gain/loss
11. intimacy or mutuality
12. breadth; depth
13. intimacy; privacy
14. particularism; concreteness
15. particularistic; immediate
16. complementarity
17. companionate
18. exclusivity
19. deficient
20. stable; internal

True/False

1. T
2. F
3. F
4. F
5. T
6. T
7. F
8. F
9. F
10. T

CHAPTER 9

Aggression and Violence

Overview

Aggression is defined as behaviour that is intended to harm or destroy. It may be used instrumentally to achieve a goal, or it may be used directly, to harm another person. There are a number of theories about what causes aggression. Some of these, psychoanalytic and ethological, assume that aggressive impulses are instinctive. Other theories postulate that there is a physiological basis to aggression. Little valid evidence is available to support these contentions. In some cases aggression is instigated by frustration. Most research emphasizes the important role of learning in the development of aggressive behaviour. Children learn how to aggress, when to aggress and against whom to aggress by social learning and by imitating models. Also, cold, punitive parents often have highly aggressive children.

There has been considerable research on the effects of viewing television violence which indicates that it increases the likelihood of violence in children and that it has long-lasting effects. Media violence may lead to increased use of weapons, it may prime aggressive acts, and it may desensitize viewers. In addition, people have copied the violent acts they have seen on television. Also, the association in the media of sex and violence may lead to violent sexual acts, especially by males.

Male and female differences in aggressive behavior may be due to hormonal levels, physique and energy levels and to learned gender roles. Aggression is expected of males whereas women are encouraged to be passive and to avoid physical encounters. However, under the appropriate conditions women can be just as aggressive as men.

Aggression can be reduced by proper child-rearing methods, especially the appropriate use of punishment. Parents and others need to learn techniques for dealing with anger. In addition, aggressive acts could be moderated by decreasing media violence, by gun control and, internationally, by effective diplomacy.

Define These Key Terms and Concepts

Twenty Questions

1. Aggression implies the _____ to harm.

2. Psychologists distinguish between _____ aggression, a
    means to a desired end, and _____ aggression, in which
    the goal is to inflict harm.

3. The _____ hypothesis states that subjects who have
    been insulted may dwell on the insult while those who have the
    opportunity to counter-aggress are distracted from the insult.
    This runs counter to the _____ hypothesis.

4. Parents who are unusually _____ and _____ tend to
    have highly aggressive sons.

5. Physically punitive parents tend to have aggressive children
    because the parent is an aggressive _____ and the parent
    may _____ aggression in the child.

6. Cross-cultural studies show that societies that are relatively small and technologically backward, make little distinction between ideal traits of "masculinity" and "femininity", enjoy eating, drinking and sexuality without guilt, and lack personalized deities tend to be relatively

   _____.

7. People who respond in a consistently aggressive manner are said to exhibit a _____ of aggressiveness.

8. An extremely violent offender with no previous history of violence may be described as a chronically _____ person.

9. In a _____ study undertaken when television was introduced into a remote community, children were found to be more _____ two years later.

10. Freedman (1984) argued that we cannot predict the effects of a "diet" of TV violence because we do not know whether the televised violence was _____.

11. Berkowitz has argued that because TV violence is paired with pleasurable experiences, aggressive behaviour may be learned through a process of _____.

12. Repeated exposure to TV violence may lead to a _____ in physiological responsiveness to violence.

13. Films such as <u>Rambo</u> may lead to mass _____ of a particular form of aggression.

14. The _____ mentality is most likely to be observed among television viewers who are authoritarians.

15. In violent pornography, _____ and _____ are associated.

16. According to the _____ theory, aggression may be intensified following sexual arousal.

17. Gender differences in aggression have been attributed to _____.

18. Favourable attitudes toward aggression are related to male _____.

19. Research shows that with regard to aggression, males and females react differently to _____ and _____.

20. A problem with generalizing from laboratory studies of aggression is that aggressive responses in an experiment may be implicitly _____.

True/False

1. Freud believed that aggression is based on the expression of the life instinct, Eros. ( )
2. Research evidence strongly supports the notion that catharsis occurs after direct or vicarious experience with aggression. ( )

3. While neurological and hormonal factors may increase emotionality and the possibility of aggression, the evidence does not support biological factors as direct causes. ( )
4. Cross-cultural studies show that violence is common in all human societies. ( )
5. Relative to other advanced industrialized states, Canada has a very low rate of violence. ( )
6. Canadian television networks carry much less violent entertainment than networks in the United States. ( )
7. People tend to watch more television in high crime areas of cities; this may account for the positive correlation between watching TV and the fear of violence. ( )
8. Viewers of aggressive pornography tend to view rape as more acceptable, and even to the point of being desired by the victims. ( )
9. Levels of male and female sex hormones have been related to levels of aggressiveness in humans. ( )
10. Male and female sex roles differ with regard to the appropriateness of aggression. ( )

Short Answer Questions

1. Distinguish between instrumental and hostile aggression, and indicate how they may have different causes.

2. What is the frustration-aggression hypothesis and how has it been reviewed by Berkowitz?

3. It is observed that subjects are less aggressive after they have committed an aggressive act: evaluate alternative explanations.

4. How can aggression be learned? Outline five aspects of the modelling of aggression.

5. How do social norms and practices encourage aggression?

6. How has the TV violence question been studied? Describe an example for each of four methods used, and indicate the limitations of each.

7. Name and describe five indirect negative consequences of media aggression.

8. Outline the excitation-transfer theory of the effects of violent pornography.

9. Are men more aggressive than women? Summarize the evidence.

10. Suggest seven ways in which a society may reduce or prevent violence.

Social Psychological Cine

All Quiet on the Western Front (Lewis Milestone, 1930)
Angels with Dirty Faces (Michael Curtiz, 1938)
Apocalypse Now (Francis Ford Coppola, 1979)
Clockwork Orange (Stanley Kubrick, 1971)
Gallipoli (Peter Weir, 1981)
Paths of Glory (Stanley Kubrick, 1975)
Persona (Ingmar Bergman, 1966)
Platoon (Oliver Stone, 1987)
Rebel Without a Cause (Nicholas Ray, 1955)
River's Edge (Tim Hunter, 1987)
Strangers on a Train (Alfred Hitchcock, 1951)
Straw Dogs (Sam Peckinpah, 1971)
Taxi Driver (Martin Scorsese, 1976)
The Confession (Costa-Gavras, 1970)
The Godfather (Francis Ford Coppola, 1972)
The Killing Fields (Roland Joffe, 1984)
War (series by Gwynn Dyer, National Film Board of Canada)
Weekend (Jean-Luc Godard, 1969)

ANSWERS

Twenty Questions

1. intent
2. instrumental; hostile
3. self-arousal; catharsis
4. punitive, rejecting
5. model; reinforce
6. peaceful and unaggressive
7. trait
8. overcontrolled
9. quasi-experimental; aggressive
10. rewarded
11. classical conditioning
12. decrease
13. contagion
14. fortress
15. sexual responses; aggressiveness
16. excitation-transfer
17. sex hormones
18. sex roles
19. aggression-eliciting cues; provocation
20. encouraged

True/False

1. F
2. F
3. T
4. F
5. F
6. F
7. T
8. T
9. T
10. T

CHAPTER 10

Altruism

Overview

This chapter deals with altruism, actions carried out with the sole purpose of helping others and without expectation of external rewards. Research has investigated a number of possible explanations for altruistic behaviour, including the possibility that some people are just "born saints" (innate predispositions), the role of a good upbringing (childrearing practices), the emotional state of the helper and the role of certain social norms. Recent studies suggest that there may be an underlying genetic predisposition to helpfulness, although it is not clear what an inherent predisposition to help others means. Altruistic actions are based to a degree on how the person makes moral judgements, and are strongly influenced by the social learning background of the person. Empathy with the person who needs help, being in a good mood and even feeling guilty or embarrassed by failure can induce altruistic behaviour. People may also help because they are responding to social norms such as feeling responsible for the welfare of others or feeling obligated to reciprocate for favours received. While a "helpful personality type" has not been discovered, variables such as culture, gender, religion and a rural or urban place of residence are related to helping in certain situations.

Much of the research in altruism has been devoted to the bystander problem, the reluctance of people to help in emergencies when other bystanders are present. The "bystander effect" occurs in situations where there is ambiguity as to whether an emergency actually exists. When we observe that others are not responding, we tend to misinterpret the situation as not involving a genuine emergency, and we also may not respond. However, when the situation is clearly an emergency, the presence of bystanders does not tend to inhibit intervention; whether and how the person will help will depend on how the person perceives the rewards and costs involved in various alternative actions. When the risks to the helper are great, heroic actions may occur, which appear to be related to a sense of adventurousness, social marginality and strong identification with the moral values and conduct of a parent.

Define These Key Terms and Concepts

Twenty Questions

1. Altruistic acts are carried out voluntarily to help others with no expectation of _____.

2. _____ is a vicarious emotional response elicited by the emotional state of someone else.

3. _____'s theory of moral development suggests that the young child behaves properly in order to win praise or avoid punishment, an older child to "look good" to others and the mature person because of personal principles.

4. When modelling influences persist over time, this suggests that altruism has been _____.

5. Models can help the child acquire two classes of prosocial behaviour: avoiding _____ acts and engaging in _____ acts which are not mandatory.

6. The _____ hypothesis suggests that people may be more likely to help someone after they experience failure than after success.

7. The norm of _____ suggests that we help those who need it, while the norm of _____ suggests that we help those who have helped us.

8. People who live in _____ are less willing than others to help.

9. The _____ effect refers to the finding that willingness to help in an emergency is reduced by the presence of other people.

10. An _____ situation is relatively rare, unpredictable, and typically involves threat or harm to someone.

11. The Darley and Latané experiment in which a "seizure" apparently occurred was a study of the _____ effect.

12. In the Darley and Latané experiment involving a "smoke-filled room", the passivity of other confederates apparently contributed to the _____ of the situation for the subject.

13. Darley and Latané's work points to three factors about the bystander effect: misperception of the _____, fear of _____ and _____.

14. In their model of bystander helping, Darley and Latané state that, after interpreting the situation as an emergency, the individual must then decide that he or she is _____ before deciding how to act.

15. The experiment in the subway car found that the bystander effect _____ occur.

16. The Piliavin "economic" model of helping assumes that as the _____ of helping increase, people will either resort to indirect helping or not helping at all.

17. The Piliavin "economic" model is most applicable in emergency situations which are _____.

18. People are more positive about those who help them when given the opportunity to _____.

19. An altruistic act involving extraordinary personal risk is considered to be _____.

20. People who acted heroically to rescue Jews from the Nazis tended to identify with a _____.

True/False

1. Most research shows that empathy is a necessary condition for altruism to occur. ( )
2. Altruism tends to increase as the child becomes older. ( )
3. Moral internalization by the child is most effectively promoted by parental withdrawal of affection as a disciplinary technique. ( )
4. After having done something which caused harm to someone, we are more likely to give help, even to someone else. ( )
5. People who help in certain situations tend to be more internal in locus of control than those who do not help. ( )
6. In situations which involve short-term interaction with strangers, men tend to help more than women. ( )
7. People who are active members of churches tend to be more altruistic than those who are not religious. ( )
8. Research on the bystander effect shows that people tend to be apathetic when witnessing an emergency. ( )
9. Studies show that the bystander effect does not occur when people cannot avoid the situation. ( )
10. People who are dependent on our help are more likely to be helped when it doesn't cost us too much. ( )

Short Answer Questions

1. Describe how prosocial behaviour has been explained in terms of the proposition that we have an innate predisposition to help others.

2. Contrast the cognitive development and social learning explanations of altruism.

3. Describe an experiment relating altruism to mood. What explanations for this relationship have been suggested?

4. Outline three norms related to helping behaviour.

5. What gender differences in altruism have been found and how are they explained?

6. How does Milgram explain differences in helping between people in big cities and small towns?

7.   What is the bystander effect and why does it occur?

8.   Compare and contrast the Latané-Darley and Piliavin models of bystander helping.

9.   How might altruistic intervention by bystanders be encouraged?

10. What is known about heroism?

Social Psychological Cine

A Tale of Two Cities (Jack Conway, 1935)
Bethune (forthcoming)
Brewster's Millions (Allan Dwan, 1945)
Christmas in July (Preston Sturgis, 1940)
Don't Cry It's Only Thunder (Peter Werner, 1982)
Magnificent Obsession (Douglas Sirk, 1954)
Silkwood (Mike Nichols, 1983)
The Scarlet Pimpernel (Clive Donner, 1982)

ANSWERS

Twenty Questions

1. external reward
2. empathy
3. Kohlberg
4. internalized
5. forbidden; desirable
6. image-repair
7. social responsibility; reciprocity
8. cities
9. bystander
10. emergency
11. bystander
12. ambiguity
13. emergency; looking foolish; diffusion of responsibility
14. personally responsible
15. did not
16. costs
17. unambiguous
18. reciprocate
19. heroic
20. moralistic parent

True/False

1. F
2. T
3. F
4. T
5. T
6. T
7. F
8. F
9. T
10. T

CHAPTER 11

Communication

Overview

This chapter is concerned with non-verbal communication and language. Non-verbal communication, such as gestures or a smile, can provide information about feelings and intentions, regulate interactions with others, express intimacy, promote social control and facilitate goal attainment. There are three different sources of non-verbal signals. First, there are facial displays many of which communicate the same information in all cultures. Second, there is body language which includes gestures and body contact. In this case there is considerable variation among cultures. The third source is called paralanguage. This refers to the non-verbal aspects of speech such as volume, pitch, speed and tone.

Both verbal and non-verbal signals are involved in almost all communication. How a message is said is often more important than what is said. In conversation words make up the content but non-verbal signals regulate the form of the conversation, such as turn-yielding, attempt-suppressing and back-channel communication.

Language is based on a phonetic system in which phonemes are combined into morphemes. Although claims have been made that some chimpanzees and gorillas have been taught to "talk" there is considerable debate as to whether they acquired a true language. None has come close to approximating the complexity of human language.

Language is an intimate part of thought and cognition. The linguistic relativity hypothesis suggests that our perception of the world is influenced by language. Language also is a crucial feature of social interaction. Speech acts can be direct, when the meaning of the sentence is consistent with the speaker's meaning, or indirect, in which this consistency is lacking. The status of those interacting will influence the choice of speech acts.

Speech style reflects a person's origin and culture. Judgements about the personality, social class, and education of individuals often are based on their style of speech. Some speech styles (standard speech), even though arbitrarily chosen, are deemed to be the most aesthetically pleasing and of higher status.

Language sets groups apart and fosters group identity. Interpersonal accommodation theory suggests that people will modify their style so as to be more similar to others when they want to obtain approval or liking (convergence). However when they want to protect their group identity they will emphasize differences in speech styles (divergence).

Bilingualism not only requires another language to be learned but other sociolinguistic skills to be acquired as well. Bilingualism can be additive when it doesn't threaten the existence of the original language or subtractive when it leads to assimilation into the majority linguistic group.

This chapter concludes with a discussion of who is capable of learning a second language. Those whose motivation is instrumental (eg., to get a better job) often do not do as well as those whose motivation is integrative (to become a part of the culture). Self-confidence also is a factor that contributes to success at second-language acquisition.

Define These Key Terms and Concepts

additive versus subtractive bilingualism	p. 398
attempt-suppressing signals	p. 375
back-channel communications	p. 375
body language	p. 369-372
communication	p. 363
conversation control	p. 374
esperanto	p. 388
facial display	p. 365-368

75

Twenty Questions

1. _____ communication usually occurs without awareness.

2. _____ may be used to signal liking, regulate

conversation and express intimacy.

3. In conversation control we rely largely on

   _____ to regulate the form of the

   conversation.

4. Chomsky argues that children must have innate predispositions

   for language since they can acquire the complex rules of

   _____ without being taught.

5. Whorf has argued that _____ determines how we think

   about the world.

6. The experiments in teaching language to apes show that, while

   they can learn words and names, they are unable to use

   _____ sentences.

7. The study by Hoffman, Lau and Johnson (1986) of the effects of

   linguistic categories on person perception showed that both

   impression and memory were affected when the target could be

   easily _____.

8. Indirect speech acts are those in which there is not a strong

   consistency between the words used and the _____

   intended by the speaker.

9. Indirect speech acts are often used to _____ in

   threatening situations.

10. _____ often functions as a cue for us to make

   inferences about the person's ethnicity, class, education and

   personality.

11. The "Ile de France" style of speaking is generally used as the _____ in assessing various styles of speaking French.

12. The _____ hypothesis states that a dialect of a language becomes the standard because it is aesthetically more pleasing than other dialects.

13. Language is a primary vehicle for group _____.

14. According to _____ theory we tend to adopt another person's way of speaking in order to gain approval and foster interaction.

15. Learning theorists argue that all humans have experiences which involve agents, actions and objects; thus there is no need to resort to an explanation in terms of _____ predispositions for grammatical rules.

16. The St. Lambert project studied the effects of _____ on subsequent proficiency in speaking French.

17. Becoming genuinely bilingual involves mastering a new set of social _____ as well as a second language.

18. Bilingualism tends to be accepted or ignored when it is _____, but resisted when it is _____.

19. People with _____ motives for learning a second language tend to be not as successful as those with _____ motives.

20.   An experiment by Segalowitz (1976) showed that subjects were

more relaxed and less anxious when spoken to in their native

English in a _____ manner, but in French in a

_____ manner.

True/False

1.   Research shows that there are basic similarities among all
     cultures in the facial expression of emotions. (   )
2.   Research shows that body language is a reliable indicator of a
     person's inner state. (   )
3.   Language is a system of communication which necessarily
     involves speech. (   )
4.   Apes are able to learn to use and combine names and to
     generalize to new instances. (   )
5.   Standard dialects, such as Parisian French, become standard
     because they are superior or more pleasing to most people.
     (   )
6.   When people interact, their ways of speaking often converge.
     (   )
7.   In Canada, according to 1981 census data, about 75% have
     English and 15% French as their mother tongue. (   )
8.   Research clearly shows that adults are much less capable than
     children of learning a second language. (   )
9.   Studies of French immersion generally show that children learn
     French with no apparent detriment to their abilities in
     English. (   )
10. People who learn a second language fluently sometimes
     experience a sense of estrangement from their own group. (   )

Short Answer Questions

1.   Outline five functions of non-verbal communication.

2. What are the ways in which eye contact can be used?

3. Is language a uniquely human ability? Outline the arguments.

4. What is the controversy between Chomsky and Skinner?

5. What is the linguistic relativity hypothesis?

6. Outline speech act theory, indicating when the types of speech acts tend to occur.

7. State the "inherent value" and "imposed norm" hypotheses about standard and non-standard dialects.

8. Explain the process of interpersonal accommodation and convergence in speaking style, and why too much convergence is not always a good thing.

9.   What is meant by sociolinguistic competence?

10.   Explain the role of motivation and aptitude in determining
      success in second-language learning.

Social Psychological Cine

      90 Days (Giles Walker, 1986)
      Being There (Hal Ashby, 1979)
      Broadcast News (James Brooks, 1987)
      Children of a Lesser God (Ronda Haines, 1986)
      Johnny Belinda (Jean Negulesco, 1948)
      Johnny got his Gun (Dalton Trumbo, 1971)

ANSWERS

Twenty Questions

1.   non-verbal
2.   eye contact
3.   non-verbal signals
4.   grammar
5.   language
6.   hierarchically structured
7.   categorized
8.   message
9.   save face
10.   speech style
11.   standard
12.   inherent value
13.   identity
14.   interpersonal accommodation
15.   innate
16.   French immersion
17.   norms
18.   additive; subtractive
19.   instrumental; integrative
20.   casual; formal

True/False

1. T
2. F
3. F
4. T
5. F
6. T
7. F
8. F
9. T
10. T

CHAPTER 12

Social Categorization, Groups and Leadership

Overview

Each of us belongs to many types of groups or social categories. The categories into which we place ourselves and other people will affect the nature of any interaction that occurs. One of the most important aspects of this subjective social ordering is the division of people into in-groups (we) and out-groups (they). Often there is some degree of resentment towards the out-group which takes the form of a generic norm. This means that we tend to automatically act in the same discriminatory manner towards all out-groups.

Social identity depends on the social categories to which a person belongs and social identification is the process whereby individuals define themselves with respect to other people. Social differentiation leads people to see members of another category as more different from themselves than they actually are, and more similar to other members of the same category than they actually are. Difficulties can arise when a person is perceived as belonging to both the in-group and an out-group. This is called cross-categorization.

When individuals feel disadvantaged relative to another category, they either attempt to assimilate with the group or to further differentiate themselves by using other criteria. In order for a social category to be a group there must be at least two people involved in interaction in which they are aware of each other and who mutually influence each other. Also, those involved in a group share common goals and the relationship is relatively stable.

One of the major reasons why people maintain group membership is cohesiveness. Cohesiveness reflects the satisfaction obtained from group membership such as goal achievement and affiliation. The group regulates the behaviour of members by requiring them to adhere to group norms. When norms are seriously violated the deviant member may be rejected.

It also has been found that groups often make decisions that are more risky than those made by individuals. This is called the risky shift effect. However, this is one aspect of group-induced attitude polarization which, under some conditions, can lead to more conservative decisions. Three explanations of polarization have been put forward: social comparison, persuasive argumentation, and social identification.

There is a distribution of power within groups. Power is a person's capacity to influence another person or group in a desired direction. There are at least seven sources of power. These are reward power, coercive power, legitimate power, expert power, informational power, referent power, and reciprocal power. The individual who has the most power in a group is usually the leader or the head. Heads are chosen from outside the group whereas leaders are selected by the group members. Leaders may have certain traits, such as height, which are hereditary and others such as intelligence, which are both innate and acquired. The situation also is important. A leader who is successful in one situation may not do well in another. Who is an effective leader, as described by the contingency model, depends on the leadership style that is most appropriate (task-oriented or socio-emotional) for the group situation.

Some leaders can be described as charismatic. They tend to be self-confident with strong convictions who provide transcendent goals and who often appear in times of stress.

Define These Key Terms and Concepts

Twenty Questions

1. Each of us belongs to many _____, such as female Canadian, student, aerobics instructor, daughter, boyfriend.

2. We tend to follow a _____ of behaviour in discriminating against all out-groups.

3. _____ refers those aspects of our self-image which depend on social categories.

84

4. Through a process of _____ we tend to see members of the same group as more similar than they really are, and members of different groups as more different than they really are.

5. If we meet someone who is a fellow student but from another country, this would be an instance of _____.

6. When we perceive ourselves as disadvantaged relative to members of another social category, we may _____ the situation to encourage favourable comparisons.

7. A group involves _____ influence, _____ over time and _____ goals.

8. A group in which the members are highly attracted to the group is described as _____.

9. Differentiation within groups occurs by means of _____ and _____.

10. Groups regulate the behaviour of members by means of _____.

11. Initial studies suggested that group decisions are more _____ than an individual's decision.

12. Subsequent research showed that group decisions tend to become more _____ relative to the initial views of members.

13. Group-induced attitude polarization has been explained in terms

    of _____ , _____ , or

    _____ .

14. The experiment by Mackie (1986), in which subjects were exposed
    to information attributed to in-group members or others,
    demonstrated the applicability of the _____
    explanation of group polarization.

15. If the power of a political leader stems from the members'
    identification with the party, this power is _____ .

16. The experiment in which subjects were assigned the roles of
    "manager" and "co-worker" showed the effects of _____
    on how people evaluate the effort of others.

17. Leaders tend to be _____ intelligent than followers.

18. Fiedler's contingency model concerns the _____ of
    leadership.

19. Leaders who rate the least-preferred co-worker negatively tend
    to be more _____ .

20. Leaders with exceptional qualities and who attract large
    numbers of committed followers are described as

    _____ .

True/False

1. Our social behaviour depends both on our individual characteristics and our social categories. (   )
2. We do not discriminate against people who are different from ourselves unless we learn a form of prejudice against that particular group. (   )
3. Crossing social categories can reduce social differentiation and in-group/out-group discrimination. (   )
4. Group cohesiveness tends to increase when there is external threat or competition. (   )
5. Group decisions are usually more risky than the decisions that individuals would make. (   )
6. The power of a professor, which derives from that role, is called legitimate power. (   )
7. Usually there is more than one leader in a group, one tending to the task and another to socio-emotional problems. (   )
8. The leader of a group is always the person elected to the position. (   )
9. Leaders tend to be relatively intelligent, self-confident and tall. (   )
10. An important characteristic of powerful, "charismatic" leaders is that they set transcendent goals for the group. (   )

Short Answer Questions

1. How is our behaviour influenced by a generic norm?

2. How do categorization and social differentiation contribute to our identity?

3. What are the effects of cross-categorization on social interaction?

4. What are the defining characteristics of a group?

5. What is the "risky shift" and how is it explained?

6. What are six bases of social power?

7. Evaluate the "great person" theory of leadership.

8. Outline Fiedler's contingency model of leadership.

9. What are the characteristics of "charismatic" leadership?

Social Psychological Cine

High Noon (Fred Zinnemann, 1952)
Lord of the Flies (Peter Brook, 1963)
Mutiny on the Bounty (Frank Lloyd, 1935)
My Beautiful Laundrette (Stephen Frears, 1985)
Red River (Howard Hawks, 1948)
The Flight of the Phoenix (Robert Aldrich, 1965)

ANSWERS

Twenty Questions

1. social categories
2. generic norm
3. social identity
4. social differentiation
5. cross-categorization
6. redefine
7. mutual; stability; shared
8. cohesive
9. roles; status
10. social norms
11. risky
12. polarized
13. social comparison; social identification; persuasion
14. social identification
15. referent
16. power
17. more
18. effectiveness
19. task-oriented
20. charismatic

True/False

1. T
2. F
3. T
4. T
5. F
6. T
7. T
8. F
9. T
10. T

CHAPTER 13

Conflict and its Resolution

Overview

Six types of conflict are identified in this chapter. These are veridical, contingent, displaced, misattributed, latent, and conflict based on false premises. We concentrate on realistic or veridical conflict where there either is competition for scarce resources, which involves incompatible goals, or incompatible principles.

One model of conflict between people is based on social exchange theory. This theory is concerned with the way in which individuals perceive the outcomes of their behaviour relative to the outcomes obtained by other people. Two standards are used to decide whether an exchange is fair, the comparison level (CL) and the comparison level for alternatives (CLalt).

Decisions about whether the distribution of resource is just or fair are based on three major rules or norms. One of these is merit or equity whereby outcomes should be relative to inputs. A second is equality whereby the resource should be distributed equally irrespective of inputs, and the third is need, whereby those who need the most get the most. Resources are of many types and can be characterized as more or less particular and more or less concrete.

The theory of game deals with two or more interdependent parties who, according to rules, make decisions that affect each other. There are two basic types of games, zero-sum and non-zero sum or mixed-motive games. The theory assumes that people act rationally in order to maximize their outcomes. Their motives may be individualistic, competitive or cooperative. A collective non-zero sum game or dilemma occurs when rational behaviour by individuals produces an outcome that is collectively undesirable.

Threats are often used in conflict situations. For a threat to be successful it must be credible. This means that the threatener must have behaved consistently in the past, that the threatened action will have negative consequences for the threatener as well as the person threatened and that the threat does not have too high a cost. Threats often escalate as a result of a threat-counter-threat spiral.

Communication which clarifies the intentions of either side can sometimes reduce conflict.

When bargaining is employed in conflict situations the most effective strategy combines firm resistance to exploitation with responsiveness to cooperative overtures.

Culture, personality traits, age, and gender have some effect on conflict behaviour but these effects often are overridden by structural variables.

Conflict often leads to the application of procedural justice using either the adversary procedure or the inquisitional procedure. The adversary procedure tends to be preferred by people because it gives them process control. This is especially the case in individualistic societies.

One means of conciliation is based on the graduated reciprocation of tension-reducing acts (GRIT). Conflict also can be reduced by the introduction of superordinate goals.

The chapter concludes with a discussion of how conflict may lead to war and contrasts two contradictory schemata that are applied in international relations: the deterrence schema and the conflict spiral schema.

Define These Key Terms and Concepts

Twenty Questions

1. When there is no basic reason for conflict between two groups (such as competition for limited resources), the conflict is considered to be _____.

2. According to _____ theory, all social interactions can be viewed as "economic" in that both sides gain rewards and incur costs.

3. In Thibaut and Kelley's model of social exchange, individuals assess their rewards and costs in terms of

_____.

4. _____ justice has to do with the fairness of outcomes, and _____ justice with the fairness of rules.

5. We may decide on the fairness of outcomes in terms of whether gains are equivalent to contributions (_____) or whether the same gains are allocated to all (_____).

93

6. Using a mediator to resolve a conflict implies a(n)

   _____ procedure of justice.

7. The theory of _____ implies a rational conflict over

   the exchange of resources in accordance with rules.

8. A two-handed game of poker is a _____ game.

9. If the purchase of an anti-pollution device on an automobile

   would be costly and not rewarding and if everyone installed

   such devices it would reduce pollution, the situation would be

   described as a _____.

10. A non-negotiable game in which goal-directed behaviour and

    threat behaviour are identical is considered to be a

    _____ game.

11. In the "trucking game" studies by Deutsch and Krauss, the

    mutual availability of _____ drastically reduced

    cooperation.

12. A _____ is a series of mutual escalating

    threats.

13. Communication was effective in increasing cooperation in the

    trucking game when subjects were given _____

    instructions.

14. The most effective strategies in eliciting cooperation are

    those in which responses match the _____ of the other

    person.

15. Conflict accompanied by _____ of the other's motives results in greater hostility.

16. The GRIT approach to conflict reduction begins with a(n)

    _____.

17. Sherif's field experiment in a boys' camp demonstrated the role of _____ in conflict reduction.

18. Sherif's study also showed that _____ was promoted by conflict between the groups.

19. Two models used to describe the arms race are _____ and _____.

20. The belief that nuclear war can be deterred if each side can destroy the other, regardless of who attacks first, is known as

    _____.

True/False

1. Conflict implies aggressive acts between two parties. (   )
2. If the CLalt is relatively high, the person will likely terminate the social exchange or relationship. (   )
3. A non-zero-sum or mixed motive game is one in which both sides can cooperate to mutual advantage. (   )
4. When a group is large, non-cooperation is the typical response in a dilemma game. (   )
5. In the Deutsch and Krauss "trucking game" study, cooperation was enhanced when both sides had the use of gates to threaten the other. (   )
6. In Western societies, competitiveness, particularly among males, increases with age. (   )
7. People disposed to be cooperative are likely to act competitively when with another competitive person. (   )
8. Superordinate goals can often cause both sides to abandon a conflict and cooperate. (   )

9. In a bargaining situation, the best strategy to bring about cooperation is either to be very tough or very generous. ( )

10. "Cooperative" people tend to behave in a way that matches the behaviour of the other side, while competitive people act competitively, regardless of the behaviour of the other. ( )

Short Answer Questions

1. Describe six types of conflict.

2. What are the two dimensions of justice, and the principles applicable to each?

3. What are the types of games and the premises underlying game theory?

4. Explain the "dilemma game" and how varying structural features such as payoff utilities can change responses.

5. What is a collective dilemma and what processes are involved?

6. What is threat in a conflict game, and what makes a threat credible?

7. What is the role of real and "illusory" power in conflict?

8. What is the role of strategy in conflict?

9. Discuss two methods to reduce conflict.

10. Contrast the deterrence and conflict spiral models of international conflict.

Social Psychological Cine

Blue Collar (Paul Schrader, 1978)
Chariots of Fire (Hugh Hudson, 1981)
FIST (Norman Jewison, 1978)
Gandhi (Richard Attenborough, 1982)
House of Strangers (Joseph L. Mankiewicz, 1949)
Norma Rae (Martin Ritt, 1979)
Personal Best (Robert Towne, 1982)
The Apartment (Billy Wilder, 1960)
The Best of Enemies (Guy Hamilton, 1962)

ANSWERS

Twenty Questions

1. unrealistic
2. social exchange
3. comparison levels
4. distributive; procedural
5. equity; equality
6. inquisitional
7. games
8. zero-sum
9. collective dilemma
10. dangerous
11. threat
12. conflict spiral
13. individualistic
14. behaviour
15. misperception
16. unilateral concession
17. superordinate goals
18. group cohesiveness
19. deterrence; conflict spiral
20. Mutually Assured Destruction

True/False

1. F
2. F
3. T
4. T
5. F
6. T
7. T
8. T
9. F
10. T

CHAPTER 14

Collective Behaviour

Overview

In this chapter, we discuss the actions which sometimes occur in large collectivities of people. These actions, which include riots, fads and fashions, mass adulation of a celebrity and social movements tend to be spontaneous, unorganized, unplanned and rather unpredictable. Basic to all of these examples is some process of "interstimulation" by which people influence each other. The behaviour of crowds has been explained in several ways: a process by which people lose a sense of individual responsibility ("deindividuation"), a "contagion" of behaviour in which people act as models to each other, and the emergence of a common set of norms which represent a consensus within the crowd about how to interpret the situation and how to react to it. Rumours, which often contribute to the reaction of crowds, tend to be distorted and are influenced by the emotional state of the participants. Fads and fashions enable people to express individuality and to differentiate people of one class, age or other social group from those of another.

Contagions refers to collective behaviours which are characterized by strong emotionality. Several have been identified: contagions of expression which provide a release of anger, joy or sorrow (mourning the death of a popular leader), contagions of enthusiasm, which often involve delusions of gaining sudden wealth ("gold fever"), contagions of anxiety ("mass hysteria") involving exaggerated concerns about some threat such as a possible epidemic, contagions of fear or panic in a situation of danger and contagions of hostility which may involve violence against scapegoats. Sometimes, collectivities of people coalesce into social movements which involve a desire for change and a conviction that something can and should be done. Often these spontaneous movements evolve into structured, organized groups such as political parties.

Define These Key Terms and Concepts

Twenty Questions

1. Collective behaviour is _____, and

    _____, _____, and involves

    _____ among the participants.

2. A _____ is unorganized, anonymous, casual and

    temporary.

3. LeBon postulated that, in some situations, a

    "_____", which is inherently irrational,

    develops in a crowd.

4. The experiment by Mann, Newton and Innes (1982) in which

    subjects simulated the audience noise in reaction to debaters

    supported _____ as an explanation of behaviour.

5. Much collective behaviour spreads through a process of

    _____.

6. Rumour transmission tends to occur in conditions of _____.

7. Rumours tend to be transmitted more when people feel

    _____.

8. _____ tend to be more important and cyclical than

    fads.

9. Fashions often serve a _____ function in

    distinguishing people of different groups and levels of

    society.

10. Fashions seem to provide some relief from _____.

11. The windshield pitting epidemic was a _____.

12. The simulation by Mintz (1951) of panic in a "bottleneck" represents the nature of panic as an _____.

13. A _____ is a spontaneous large group constituted in support of shared purposes.

14. Social movements may be nationalistic, political or _____ in nature.

15. Often, successful social movements become _____ and end up as a part of mainstream society.

16. Most cults are organized around a _____ leader.

17. An all-encompassing _____ is the major tool of many cults in attracting and keeping its members.

18. Zimbardo's simulated prison study supports the role of _____ in behaviour.

19. In the Rocket Richard hockey riot of 1955, an _____ crowd became an _____ crowd.

20. The voting behaviour of the majority of individuals is _____ from one election to the next.

True/False

1. Collective behaviour is relatively common in situations such as hockey games or on crowded buses. (   )
2. The evidence shows that some crowd situations release undesirable human instincts. (   )
3. Over time, rumours often tend to grow less detailed, more exaggerated and consistent with the assumptions of people. (   )
4. Fashions often serve to distinguish people belonging to different social classes. (   )
5. Collective behaviours in which people want to cheer a Pope, hockey team or political leader are contagions of expression. (   )
6. The Yorkville hepatitis epidemic was, in reality, a contagion of enthusiasm. (   )
7. One can usually predict when an aggressive crowd is likely to form. (   )
8. Social movements are usually political in nature. (   )
9. Cults usually provide members with a sense of freedom and a great deal of flexibility in their lives. (   )
10. Most voters in elections respond in terms of self-interest or group interests, rather than political ideology. (   )

Short Answer Questions

1. What are the four defining characteristics of collective behaviour?

2. Describe and criticize the contagion theory of crowd behaviour.

3. What are the five conditions for deindividuation?

4. Outline emergent norm theory and contrast it with contagion theory and deindividuation.

5. According to Allport and Postman, what are the three processes in the transformation of rumours?

6. Name and define four types of contagions.

7. Describe a case study of a contagion of anxiety.

8. Describe a case study of a contagion of fear, and the processes.

9. What are the stages in the development of a social movement?

10. What were three social psychological processes observed in the Jonestown incident?

Social Psychology Cine

A Face in the Crowd (Elia Kazan, 1957)
Elmer Gantry (Richard Brooks, 1960)
Fury (Fritz Lang, 1936)
Gimme Shelter (Al and David Maysles, 1970)
Hail the Conquering Hero (Preston Sturgis, 1944)
Lord of the Flies (Peter Brook, 1963)
The Children's Hour (William Wyler, 1962)
The Devils (Ken Russell, 1971)
The Ox-Bow Incident (William Wellman, 1943)
The Song of Bernadette (Henry King, 1943)
Woodstock (Michael Wadleigh, 1970)

ANSWERS

Twenty Questions

1. relatively spontaneous; unorganized;
   unplanned; interstimulation
2. crowd
3. "collective mind"
4. deindividuation
5. contagion
6. uncertainty
7. anxious
8. fashions
9. status-marking
10. banality
11. contagion of anxiety
12. N-person game
13. social movement
14. religious
15. institutionalized
16. charismatic
17. belief system
18. deindividuation
19. expressive; aggressive
20. consistent

True/False

1. F
2. F
3. T
4. T
5. T
6. F
7. F
8. F
9. F
10. T

CHAPTER 15

Social Psychology and Social Problems

Overview

This chapter discusses the application of social psychology to the understanding and solution of social problems. Early optimism about the efficacy of applying social psychology has been tempered in recent years by an awareness of problems to personal rather than social causes and the implicit value of self-contained individualism. Nonetheless, social psychology remains a discipline which is involved in social issues. In the area of the law, research has focused on eyewitness testimony and identification, the process of giving testimony, and the dynamics of jury decisions. Eyewitness recall is often affected by factors such as the race of the protagonist, and stressful circumstances as well as lighting, distance and the time elapsed between the event and the recall or identification. The testimony of eyewitnesses can be influenced by how the questions are asked of the witness. Mock jury studies suggest that jury decisions may be affected by psychological characteristics of jurors such as authoritarianism, the size of the jury (smaller juries are more likely to convict) and even the introduction of evidence which is ruled as inadmissible.

Social psychological research on the physical environment has considered a wide variety of topics. Environmental stressors such as noise, excessive heat and crowding can disrupt performance and even affect health in the long run, particularly when they are experienced as unpredictable or beyond the control of the person. Physical density cannot be equated with the subjective feeling of being crowded, and, indeed, high density situations tend to intensify both positive and negative experiences (for example, a crowded subway and a crowd at a ball game). In crowded situations such as in large cities, we tend to "turn off", avoiding or ignoring much of what is happening around us in order to reduce the level of stimulation. People will tend to behave in ways beneficial to the environment, such as by conserving energy or not littering, when the perceived benefits exceed the costs and when the "trade-off" of environmental and economic benefits can be resolved. The design of buildings and working or living areas has been influenced by research on the behavioural effect of design.

Studies of how people are reacting to the threat of a nuclear war reveal a variety of reactions, including denial, apathy, resignation and activism. Those who are most concerned are more likely to show signs of depression, but are also more likely to become politically active in order to try to affect the outcome. Activists tend to think of nuclear war in vivid and concrete images, rather than political or numerical abstractions. Widely-disseminated films about the aftermath of a nuclear war have had a minimal impact on public attitudes, although they did bring the issue into the consciousness of many, and may have generated political action by some.

Define These Key Terms and Concepts

Twenty Questions

1. The objective, data-based assessment of a social program is

    called _____.

2. In much of applied research, an attributional bias is evident

    in that social problems are attributed primarily to

    _____.

3. Lewin's idea of action research involves using research data in

    order to _____.

4. _____ personalities are more likely to convict and to

    recommend severe sentences.

5. Subjects exposed to noise are more likely to behave

    aggressively against someone unless they believe that the noise

    is _____.

6. The Calhoun study in which rats were permitted to procreate

    within a fixed space supports the _____

    hypothesis.

7. Milgram argues that one of the effects of urban crowding is

   _____.

8. Research by Freedman and others shows that high-density

   situations _____ our usual reactions in those

   situations.

9. When subjects in a high-density situation are provided with a

   button to press if they "want out", the effects of high density

   are less _____.

10. Actions consistent with people's concerns about the environment

    may be inhibited by the _____ dilemma.

11. In the study of university residence design by Baum and

    colleagues (1978), it was found that students living in

    _____ were more sociable than those living in

    corridor arrangements.

12. Because a nuclear war would be unexpected as well as

    catastrophic, collective reactions of _____ and

    _____ are to be expected.

13. Public concern about nuclear threat tends to increase during

    periods of _____.

14. Consistent attitudes toward the threat of nuclear war and

    toward possible accidents from nuclear reactors reveal an

    underlying _____.

15. Studies of children show that those who are most preoccupied with the nuclear threat also believe that they can _____ it in some way.

16. Anti-nuclear activists tend to attribute war and peace to _____ and _____, while survivalists attribute them _____.

17. Studies of the effects of the film <u>The Day After</u> showed immediate increases in _____ of the problem.

18. In general, research in social psychology has been characterized by reciprocal, two-way influences between the _____ and _____.

19. Studies of the effects of lowering the minimum drinking age show relatively high increases in _____ among _____.

20. Studies of attitudes toward capital punishment show the _____ motive to be a primary motive for the support of capital punishment.

True/False

1. Action research involves attempts to effect social change. (　)
2. Eyewitness testimony is generally accurate if the eyewitness is sure of what he or she witnessed. (　)
3. Research shows a causal link between lowering the drinking age and the number of alcohol-related traffic fatalities. (　)
4. The research on jury size shows that a twelve-person jury is unnecessary to secure a fair trial. (　)
5. Studies of violence in large U.S. cities show that violence increases when the temperature is high. (　)
6. Population density refers to the discomfort accompanying the perception that there are too many people. (　)
7. Males tend to react more positively than females in high-density situations. (　)
8. Students living in residential suites tend to be more friendly than those in conventional residences, even when outside of the residence. (　)
9. Studies of the effects of a film depicting the aftermath of a nuclear war show long-term changes in attitudes and actions. (　)
10. Research has uncovered surprising evidence of the effects of phases of the moon upon behaviour. (　)

Short Answer Questions

1. Outline the principles and difficulties in doing research on socially-relevant problems.

2. What are the effects of leading questions on eyewitness testimony?

3. Evaluate the internal and external validity of simulated jury studies.

4. What are the arguments against reducing the size of a jury from twelve to six?

5. Relate the effects of various stressors to controllability or predictability.

6. What are the characteristics of interior design that seem to increase social interaction?

7. What are the basic attitudinal reactions to the nuclear threat, and what psychological correlates of these reactions have been reported?

8. Explain the effects of the film <u>The Day After</u>.

9. Describe the various reactions of children to the nuclear threat.

10. What are the indicators of "quality of life"?

Social Psychological Cine

Dr. Strangelove (Stanley Kubrick, 1964)
Fail-Safe (Sidney Lumet, 1964)
If you Love this Planet (Terri Nash, 1982)
On the Beach (Stanley Kramer, 1959)
Testament (Lynne Littman, 1983)
The China Syndrome (James Bridges, 1979)
The Conversation (Francis Ford Coppola, 1974)
The Day After (Nicholas Meyer, 1984)
The War Game (Peter Watkins, 1967)
The Wrong Man (Alfred Hitchcock, 1956)
Twelve Angry Men (Sidney Lumet, 1957)
Vertigo (Alfred Hitchcock, 1958)

ANSWERS

Twenty Questions

1. evaluation research
2. persons
3. influence change
4. authoritarian
5. controllable
6. social pathology
7. sensory overload
8. magnify
9. stressful
10. trade-off
11. suites
12. panic; hysterical contagion
13. international crises
14. nuclear anxiety
15. control
16. government; the public; uncontrolled forces
17. awareness or availability
18. laboratory; real-life
19. alcohol-related accidents; 19-20-year-olds
20. retribution

True/False

1. T
2. F
3. T
4. F
5. F
6. F
7. F
8. T
9. F
10. F

CHAPTER 16

Health and Illness

Overview

This chapter reviews work in three areas relevant to health: the behavioural and psychological factors which constitute a risk to health, the personal and social implications of being ill and ways in which health can be promoted and disease prevented. Among adolescents, behaviours which represent a health risk, such as alcohol and drug abuse and sexual promiscuity, form part of a pattern or "syndrome" of non-conventional characteristics of personality, the peer environment and behaviour. These behaviours are also subject to the influence of modelling by both peers and parents. Those who are most vulnerable to illness tend to lack the support of others and also lack a sense of personal control. In the case of coronary diseases, people at risk tend to be highly competitive, impatient and rather hostile.

When people are seriously ill, they tend to assume a social role. That is, they tend to act as others expect them to act, and to be perceived in ways which may isolate them from others and even to prolong the illness. Communication between patient and physician, such as when expressing pain, must be seen in the context of the role of being a patient or being ill. Other research shows that most patients tend to recover more readily and to comply with the recommendations of their physicians when they are fully informed about their health problems and possible solutions by their physician.

Health promotion is aimed both at primary prevention (reducing the chance of contracting the disease or condition) and secondary prevention (early detection and treatment to minimize the risk to health). Fear arousal may be effective in eliciting better health behaviours when it is not excessive and when presented along with recommendations for a realistic and effective behavioural response to the threat. The health beliefs model concerns how people make decisions relevant to their health, such as exercising, losing weight, quitting smoking or taking appropriate medication as directed. According to the model, such decisions are based on the perception of a serious and personal threat to health, awareness of specific cues to take action and accessibility of actions in which the perceived benefits outweigh the costs. However, many of our actions which implicate our health do not involve conscious decisions. And, even after people change their habitual behaviours relevant to their health, relapse is common unless the person is equipped to deal with high-risk situations and does not interpret a slip as an absolute failure.

Define These Key Terms and Concepts

Twenty Questions

1. In the twentieth century in industrialized nations, there has
    been a shift in concern from _____ diseases to
    _____ diseases.

2. Problem behaviour theory involves a pattern of _____,
    _____ and _____ characteristics.

3. Problems with alcohol are related to the amount of alcohol
    consumed (of course) and also to factors such as the use of
    _____.

4. People who drink with a heavy drinker tend to drink more
    because of _____ influences.

5. Social support may not always be beneficial to health because
    others may _____ the person from the consequences of
    maladaptive behaviour.

6.   Studies show that many women in contemporary society react adversely to a(n) _____ conception of what is "fat".

7.   The research of Langer and Rodin (1976) with elderly residents in a nursing home shows the importance of _____ for health.

8.   People with an _____ locus of control tend to take care of themselves and cope better with illness.

9.   Staying in bed, not working, and having others care for you are all part of the _____.

10.   People of different cultures often _____ pain differently.

11.   The MUM effect refers to the reluctance of physicians to communicate _____ to the patient.

12.   In a study by Johnson and Leventhal (1974) concerning people about to undergo an uncomfortable endoscopic examination found that they adapted better to the discomfort (e.g., less gagging) when provided with _____ beforehand.

13.   When patients perceive that their physician is friendly and interested in them, they are more likely to _____.

14.   Primary prevention refers to reducing the rate of onset of a disease, while secondary prevention refers to _____.

15. If a person believes that coronary disease is serious, that he or she is susceptible and that the recommended action would be effective, then persuasion which involves _____ would produce better health practices.

16. Community programs which involve _____ tend to have beneficial effects.

17. The health beliefs model deals with the relationship between health-related _____ and _____ .

18. In the health beliefs model, the perception of a personally relevant threat from illness leads to behaviour change if there are _____ .

19. The abstinence violation effect involves _____ and _____ attributions.

20. A major flaw with the health beliefs model is that it assumes a _____ process of decision-making.

True/False

1. People engage in behaviours which are health risks primarily because of various addictions. (   )
2. Results from Jessor's longitudinal study of adolescent problem behaviour show that those who are problem drinkers as adults usually began to show such problems in adolescence. (   )
3. While the rate of problem drinking is higher among males than females, females who drink heavily are more likely to manifest problems. (   )
4. People in pubs drink more in large groups because they spend a longer period of time in the pub. (   )
5. People who lack supportive bonds with others are more likely to suffer illness and less likely to recover quickly. (   )

6. When people are seriously ill, their illness usually brings them closer to others in their lives. (   )
7. Research shows that around 20% of patients do not even bother to have prescriptions filled. (   )
8. Patients with hypertension usually comply with their physician's recommendations because they can detect when their blood pressure is elevated. (   )
9. Laws which require the use of automobile seatbelts result in reduced traffic fatalities. (   )
10. People who have lost a spouse are more likely to die in the immediate period afterwards. (   )

Short Answer Questions

1. Outline the three systems in Jessor's problem behaviour theory, and give two variables from each system.

2. Describe the relationship between social support and health.

3. What personality factors are related to health and recovery from illness?

4. What is the role schema for being sick and what adaptive tasks must be faced?

5. What is the "patient compliance" problem and what can be done about it?

6. Contrast primary and secondary prevention.

7. What are three strategies to prevent health-risk behaviours among adolescents?

8. Outline the health beliefs model.

9. Why is maintenance of behaviour change such a major problem in health promotion?

10. What are Janis' five alternatives regarding coping with health-related decisions?

Social Psychological Cine

All That Jazz (Robert Fosse, 1979)
Britannia Hospital (Lindsay Anderson, 1982)
Hospital (Frederic Wiseman, 1978)
On Golden Pond (Mark Rydell, 1981)
Terms of Endearment (James Brooks, 1984)
The Days of Wine and Roses (Blake Edwards, 1962)
The Lost Weekend (Billy Wilder, 1945)
Whose Life is it, Anyway? (John Badham, 1981)

ANSWERS

Twenty Questions

1. infectious; chronic
2. personality; environmental; behavioural
3. other drugs
4. modelling
5. protect
6. unrealistic
7. perceived control
8. internal
9. sick role schema
10. interpret
11. bad news
12. information
13. comply
14. early detection
15. fear arousal
16. health education
17. attitudes; behaviours
18. cues for action
19. stable; personal
20. rational

True/False

1. F
2. F
3. T
4. T
5. T
6. F
7. T
8. F
9. T
10. T

122